tr
Family Tree

BROCKHAMPTON PRESS
LONDON

Contents

Introduction

Many people have, as schoolchildren, been asked to find out information about their immediate families and to compile a basic 'family tree', giving the dates of birth of brothers, sisters, parents, aunts, uncles, cousins and grandparents. In some families, separated by distance, feuds or death, this in itself can prove quite a challenge. Further research can, therefore, be somewhat more complicated. The rewards that can be reaped from a detailed search of one's family history, however, can be quite considerable and well worth the time and effort that must be spent.

We may think that we are ordinary people from ordinary families, but some people will be quite surprised when they look back in time to see what their great-great-grandparents did for a living, or find out that they are directly descended from some important figure in history. Even if your research only proves that you do come from an 'ordinary' family—if indeed there is such a thing—then you will have given yourself a much clearer picture of your roots and your identity, and the records that you have made will be something to pass on through further generations as your family carries on. Names and dates are only the start of what can become a fascinating journey of discovery into the past.

Do not embark upon your project without being prepared to spend quite a lot of time and patience working on it. Your search for your ancestors may uncover connections with foreign countries. You will very possibly follow false leads. If your family name is a relatively common one, you will have more work to do to eliminate people that have the same name but are unrelated.

Nevertheless, you should not be willing to give up too easily. Genealogy is a popular study, and there are many organizations and reference sources that can be of help to you. If you do get stuck at any point, there are people who could take on part of your search for you, for a fee, although this can prove rather costly. If you do feel that you could do with some help, or simply some guidance and encouragement in your studies, a cheaper alternative might be to enquire from your library or local education authority for adult education classes on the subject. Many local authorities run classes on genealogy. If your search is confined to your own country, or even your own district, a locally organized class will provide you with the best information on researching family histories in your area, but you should find that you will also be given invaluable advice on conducting a search further afield. If no such class exists, then you could suggest that such a course be put on the curriculum for the following session.

If you have reason to believe that your family has lived in the same area for several generations, you may also find it helpful to join a local history society. Such a group can help to provide you with interesting background information about the sort of society in which your forebears lived. If your family was well known in the area, it may well be that some work has been done on aspects of your family's history already.

It is also a good idea to check at your local library to see if there is in existence a family history society in your area. Recently, many of these have sprung up all over the country, and if you find that there is not such a society locally, why not think about starting one up. Not only can such societies help with the exchange of information and techniques among members, but they can also help one keep one's enthusiasm for what can sometimes seem a daunting task. Most local family history societies belong to the Federation of Family History Societies (the address is given on page 60), a national organization that publishes useful, inexpensive guides and its own magazine, *Family History News and Digest*. Some local societies produce their own journals and publish editions of some local records, such as census returns.

Your aim is to record the most important details about your family in a concise form, but you will probably find that your research uncovers a whole host of information that you will need to sift through before you can condense it into the record. It is advisable, therefore, to make a separate collection of records first. When you have assembled all your information, you will have a much clearer idea of the details that you wish to note down.

Record Keeping

From the very start, keep your records organized and tidy, with a separate section for each person in the family. A card index system or loose-leaf file, which can be added to as more information comes to light, is ideal. Although you will probably want to keep much of the information that you have gathered in note form, do be careful to ensure that your notes are clear and concise. Abbreviations and initials may appear to be perfectly comprehensible at the time of writing, but they have to be able to stand the test of time. Will you still remember what they stand for when you come back to them after weeks, or months? If you are one of the many people who now have a personal computer or word processor, you can record your information electronically, although unless you have a laptop computer, you will have to take notes as you go along and type the information up later. There are computer programs available to help you put your information in a standard form.

As in so many other areas, the instant access to global information provided by the Internet is likely to prove a great boon, particularly if you are seeking information on foreign ancestors. There are already hundreds of genealogical files on the Internet, and the number is certain to increase greatly. As the range of historical information increases so will the Internet revolutionize the task of someone wishing to know more.

You will probably want to draw up a family tree, or at least some sort of chart, containing the most basic information such as dates of births, marriages and deaths. A basic chart is provided, but you may wish to devise one of your own as well, to fulfil your own particular requirements. There are no specific rules as to how such a chart should be compiled, but it is important to keep the information down to the bare minimum for clarity, and there should be plenty of space for additions to be made as necessary. It is traditional to trace a family tree back through the male line, but you should feel no compunction to do this, or even to stop at this. It is entirely up to you which, and how many, 'branches' of your own family tree you choose to follow.

Be accurate in recording any information you come

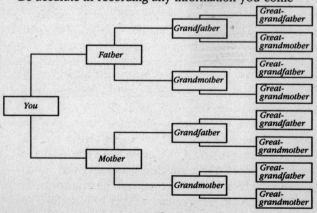

across. If you find documents relating to a particular person or event, note down the information that the documents contain carefully and make a note of the source. Accuracy helps to avoid confusion.

Keep a record of absolutely everything that you find out. Whether or not it appears relevant to you at that particular stage in your research, it may still be useful at a later date. If you find records that may relate to your family but that you cannot prove to do so, then make a note of them as such; further research may bring the proof that you require to light.

Be meticulous in checking your facts. Try at all times to have all the information that you collate checked against official sources.

Finally, remember that the broader the scope of your search, the fuller the picture will be that you build up of your family through the years.

First Steps

Start with yourself and your immediate family. Note down details of your own birth date and place, your parents' names, including your mother's maiden name, the address of your first and any later homes, and any details that you consider to be relevant to your life so far. Next, do the same for any brothers or sisters and their children, your spouse, your children and grandchildren, if applicable. Find out all you can about your parents' families; their parents, their siblings, and, if any, their siblings' children. The inclusion of family photographs, letters, etc, in your records is a matter of personal choice, but these can make the family history all the more interesting for future readers. A collection of family photographs spanning two, three or even four generations will be quite fascinating; you may be surprised to find out how 'family features' have been passed down through the generations, or how even fairly distant relatives can bear a resemblance to each other!

Copies of birth certificates and other public records should be included; these are vital pieces of evidence.

If there are any newspaper cuttings of interest and relevance to your family, add these to your records.

When you have made a note of all the information

that is immediately to hand, you can begin to widen your search. Ask among all your relatives, particularly elderly ones, for any details about more distant family members. Tell them all that you know so far. You may have some information upon which someone else can elaborate, but about which they might have forgotten.

Note down everything that you are told, but be careful to check everything as far as possible to make sure that the facts are correct. Dates and places can become muddled over a long period of time, and while memories can act as pointers in your search for the past, they cannot be relied upon.

Did any of the menfolk serve in either of the World Wars? In which branch of the services did they serve? Were there any awards for bravery? If you are given any information about serving men such as the above, it can lead you on to further searches of service records, war memorials, newspaper archives, etc.

Is there a family grave? Where is it? A visit to the graveyard can be very helpful.

Make a thorough search for family memorabilia. Someone may have an old photograph album that contains family photographs dating back some years. See how many of the people in the photographs can be identified. Find out if anyone has any old certificates of baptism, school records, burial cards or other documents that could help to fill in details of past family members. Letters, bills, accounts and diaries may have been kept in the attic of some elderly aunt for years; old books may contain interesting inscriptions. Anything that has a date on it, or that can be dated, can help you to place your family at certain points in time.

If you have emigrated or moved away from the area in which your family lived for generations, contact with any of your relatives who still live in the area will be of even more importance. Although you may not be in a position to visit family members living abroad or in other parts of the country, you can always write to them and ask for their help, enclosing a list of questions that they may be able to answer. If your surname is a relatively uncommon one, and you know the area from which your family originated but are unsure whether any family members still live there, it may be possible to try a similar approach. Look up a local telephone directory to find people in the area who share the same surname, and write to them expressing your intentions and asking them if they are willing to assist you. Your enquiries may reveal that none of these people is in fact related to your family; indeed, you may find that the people to whom you write are not willing to help at all! Nevertheless, there is always a possibility of discovering interesting family connections.

You may find that someone in your family has already done some research, or has kept some records that can be of help to you. Remember, however, that it is essential to check everything. If you have, or one of your family has, a family bible in their possession, this can be a very useful source of information. It was once customary to record details of births and deaths in the family bible, and these records can provide valuable information as to where to look next in your search.

Very quickly you will find that as your known forebears multiply, so also do the avenues of investigation that can be followed. It is advisable to be selective at first and to concentrate your efforts in one direction at a time. More information about other branches of the family will undoubtedly come to light as your work progresses. Note this down for future reference, but try not to be diverted from the task in hand, as this can lead to confusion.

Since abbreviations are a necessary part of family trees, you will find it sensible to use those abbreviations that are standard in genealogy. Some of these are listed below for guidance:

b.	born
bpt	baptised
d.	died
d. unm.	died unmarried
d.s.p.	died without children (Latin *decessit sine prole*)
dau.	daughter
s.	son
div.	divorced
unm.	unmarried
=	married
l	left descendants

Official Records: Registers of Births, Marriages and Deaths

Once you have found out all you can from your family, you will have to move on to searching through public records. This is advisable for checking any details about your family that have been given to you without documentary evidence to back them up. Moreover, it will be necessary to search the public records for details of your family further back in time.

One of the most useful sources of information is the National Register of births, marriages and deaths. Civil registers for England and Wales have been kept since 1837. In Scotland and Ireland, the registers began later, in 1855 and 1864 respectively. Although this does not take you very far back in time, it will help you to fill out some details. For example, birth records will give details of the child's parents' names and the mother's maiden name. Thus, even the earliest entry that you can find for your family in the registers will give you clues for your search into the more distant past. The registers will also give the name and address of the person who went to make the entry and this too can be useful, if that person was another family member.

England and Wales
Registers of births, deaths and marriages are all recorded

locally and centrally. The central records are all kept in the Office of Population Censuses and Surveys, General Register Office, St Catherine's House, London. If you wish to conduct a search there, admission is free, but you are not permitted to look at the original registers. Instead, you have to make a search of the indexes to find the entry that you are looking for, after which you can apply for a copy of the relevant certificate, for a fee.

The indexes to the births, marriages and deaths are arranged on shelves with a separate section for each, the sections being arranged chronologically. Up to 1984, the indexes are compiled in quarters. Thus, the March index for any particular year includes entries for January, February and March; the June index entries for April, May and June, the September index entries for July and August, and the December index entries for October and November. From 1984, the indexes are compiled for the full year. The surnames of the entries are alphabetical within each quarter or year, with the forenames arranged alphabetically under the surname.

Also given in the index is the name of the Superintendent Registrar's District. Books indicating the location of these registration districts are available at the front desk of the General Register Office, or you can obtain from the Society of Genealogists a booklet by Ray Wiggins entitled *St Catherine's House Districts*, which contains an alphabetical list of the original districts, around 650. If you know which registration district you are likely to be interested in, you will save time and effort when consulting the indexes.

If you are planning a trip to St Catherine's House, make sure you are well prepared with as much information as possible about the person or persons for whose records you are searching.

Births

If you are searching for a birth entry before 1875, do not be surprised if you cannot find it. In 1875, legal penalties were introduced to enforce the registration of births, but before then, it was quite common for people to leave births unregistered.

A period of 42 days was permitted in which the parents had to register the birth of their child, so the birth may be registered in a later index.

Remember that it costs money to obtain a certificate, so be sure that there are no 'doublers' to eliminate before you make any costly mistakes. If you are searching for the birth of a John Smith in October 1895, you may find another John Smith born at the same time. If you know of any second forename of your John Smith this will help. The registration district is another vital piece of information. If you know where your John Smith was born, you are much more likely to be able to find the right one.

The earlier birth indexes contain only the names of the child, the district of registration and the date of birth. Records made from September 1911 to the present day, however, contain the maiden name of the child's mother, which makes the search for more recent ancestors considerably easier.

Deaths

As with births, the registration of deaths may not have taken place in the same quarter as that in which death occurred. It may be necessary, therefore, to search the index for the quarter in which the death occurred and the index for the subsequent quarter.

Up until 1866, there are not many clues to be gleaned from the death indexes themselves. Only the name of the deceased, the district of registration and the relevant page and volume numbers for the register are given.

From the March quarter of 1866 onwards, the age of the deceased at death is given, as supplied by the person registering the death. This can help in the search for dates of birth, but bear in mind that it may not be accurate.

Indexes from the June quarter 1969 onwards show the date of birth of the deceased, where known.

Marriages

From 1837 until the end of 1911, marriage indexes show only the surname of the person for whom the entry was made. In order to confirm that the index reference you have found is the correct one, it is necessary to find the index entries for both parties and check that the page numbers for the register tally. In order to do this, you must, of course, know both the surname of the man and the maiden name of the woman.

Indexes after and including that of March 1912 show the surnames of second parties to marriage alongside the first names and surnames of the person for whom the entry was made.

Certificates: How To Get Them And What They Tell You

Searching the indexes at St Catherine's House is free, but there is a fee to be paid for obtaining a certificate once you have found the relevant index entry.

You can apply for certificates in person at St Catherine's House. Provided that you have been able to supply all the necessary information, the certificate that you have requested will be sent to you within a few days, or you may collect it in person, if you prefer. There is a priority service available at St Catherine's House, which provides certificates within 24 hours, but this service is considerably more expensive.

You can also apply for certificates by post. The address for postal applications is given on page 60. This service is slower, but provided the details supplied are adequate, the relevant certificate is usually sent off within 28 days.

Birth certificates

A full birth certificate will supply you with the following information:

- The name and date of birth of the child
- The address of the child
- The name and occupation, at the time of registration,

of the child's father—where the child was illegitimate there may be a blank space where the father's name should be
- The name and maiden name of the child's mother
- The date of registration of birth
- The district of registration
- The name and address of the person supplying the information to the registrar

Death certificates
Death certificates will tell you:
- The names and address of the deceased
- The place of death
- The cause of death
- The date and place of registration of death, and the name and address of the person supplying the information
- If the deceased was a man or a single woman, the certificate lists his or her occupation
- If the deceased was a married woman, the name and occupation of her husband are given
- If the deceased was a child, the name and occupation of the father are given

Marriage certificates
A marriage certificate contains the following information:
- The names of the male party, and age at time of marriage, but you should note that many marriage certificates before 1870 do not specify the age but record the fact that the relevant person was 'of full

age', a term that does not necessarily indicate the age of 21, the birthday that the phrase 'coming of age' used to mean, or the age of 18, the birthday that the term now signifies, but sometimes simply 'the age of consent', a then unspecified age that, until 1929, might have been even lower than the age of 16

- The marital status of the male party (bachelor, widower or divorcee)
- The address and occupation of the male party, and his father's name and occupation (the certificate will also indicate whether or not the father was still alive at the time of the event)
- The names of the female party, her age, address, marital status and occupation at time of marriage
- The name and occupation of her father
- The names of witnesses to the marriage ceremony
- The place where the marriage ceremony was performed

Each certificate provides its own set of clues to help you in further searches. With death certificates, for example, the cause of death may be enlightening. Was it an accident, or something that might have been reported in the newspapers? If so, it might be worth a search in newspaper archives.

Who were the witnesses to marriages? Were they relatives or friends?

Who supplied the information to the registrar for births and deaths? Were they related?

You find that somebody has been married before.

When was it, and how long did the marriage last? Did that marriage produce any children?

You might find out that a man is listed as a carpenter, or has some other occupation for which he may have served an apprenticeship. Is there a possibility that someone in the family is in possession of his apprenticeship indentures?

Follow every clue that you are given; any information that you come up with may be of value to you.

Other records

There are other records available for consultation at St Catherine's House if you find that your search is leading towards anything more specific or unusual. These records include the following:

- Consular returns: records of births, deaths and marriages registered abroad by British consuls, from 1849
- High Commission returns: births, deaths and marriages registered by British High Commissions in most Commonwealth countries from 1947
- Registers of deaths of servicemen and women in the First and Second World Wars
- General records of births, deaths and marriages abroad
- Register of births and deaths at sea from 1837: any births or deaths occurring on ships registered in Great Britain
- Register of births and deaths in aircraft: these records date from 1949 and relate to events occurring on any British-registered aircraft

- The Adopted Children's Register: this contains records of all adoptions made under court order in England and Wales since 1927. A full certificate will give the names of the adoptive parents, as well as the date of the adoption order. Short certificates give no reference to adoption

Register of Births, Marriages and Deaths in Scotland

The central source of information in Scotland is New Register House in Edinburgh.

As at St Catherine's House, you are permitted to search the indexes but at New Register House a fee is charged.

Indexes at New Register House are compiled by the year, and male and female entries are kept separate. The indexes will give you the name of the registration district. Each district is assigned a number in the register and this has, in some cases, changed over the years, but there are charts available that will tell you the number of the registration district you require for the relevant year. You need the same amount of information as in England for searching the indexes, but having found the entry or entries that you seek, and having noted the number for the registration district, you are then able to apply to see the register itself. This can save unnecessary expense, for you are more likely to establish whether you have found the right certificate before you make any purchases. Bear in mind that there may be a considerable wait before you are provided with the register book that you have asked for. New Register House is a busy place, and there may be a queue. For the same reason, the time that you are permitted to spend studying the register may be limited.

If you need to go to New Register House to consult the records, you would be well advised to plan your visit carefully to avoid wasting time and money. Be as sure as you can be about what you are looking for before you go.

You can book a seat in the search room in advance over the telephone, but if you have not booked, try to arrive at 9.30 a.m., when the Search Rooms open, in order to ensure a place for yourself.

Indexes

The index of births contains the child's name, the name of the registration district, and the number of entry in the register.

The index of deaths supplies the name of the deceased, the registration district, the entry number, and after 1865, the age of the deceased at death. Early indexes will list a married woman under her married name, and her maiden name will also be supplied. Indexes after 1865 will always list a married woman twice, once under her maiden name and once under her married name. If she has been married more than once, an entry should appear for each of her married names, although this is not always the case.

The marriage indexes for 1855–1863 list the parties to the marriage separately, as in England, but the woman's married name is given alongside her maiden name. After this, it is necessary to find the index for the woman under her maiden name, and cross-reference this with the index for the husband in order to check that the entries coincide in the register.

Certificates

Copies of certificates of birth, death or marriage may be obtained from New Register House either by applying in person, or by applying by post or fax. Personal applications are the cheaper alternative, and the service is generally quicker, with certificates being sent off to you within approximately five working days. Applications by telephone are not accepted.

Birth certificates

Scottish birth certificates contain the following information:

- The child's name and address
- The date, place and time of birth
- The names of the child's parents
- The maiden name of the mother
- The occupation of the father
- The date and place of marriage of the child's parents with the exception of the years 1856–1860
- The name and signature of the informant

Death Certificates

Death certificates will furnish you with the following:

- The name and occupation of the deceased
- Marital status of the deceased, and, after 1859, where applicable, the name of the spouse
- Date, place and cause of death

- Names of the parents of the deceased, whether alive or dead, and occupation of the father of the deceased
- Name of the informant, and relationship of the informant to the deceased

Other Records

Apart from the registers of births, marriages and deaths and the census records and parish records (which will be discussed later in this book), New Register House in Edinburgh also contains the following records that can be of use to the amateur or professional genealogist:

- Register of Neglected Entries (1801–1854): this register records births, deaths and marriages that took place in Scotland between 1801 and 1854 but that were omitted from the parish registers
- Register of Adopted Children (1930 onwards): this register records all adoptions made under order of the Scottish courts
- Register of Divorces (after May 1984): this records the names of both parties, dates and places of marriage and divorce, and details of court orders relating to custody of and financial provision for any children in any divorces granted by the Scottish courts
- Marine Register of Births and Deaths (from 1855): this register records births and deaths at sea on any British-registered merchant vessel, anywhere in the world, where the child has one or both parents considered to be Scottish residents, and the deceased is a Scottish resident
- Air Register (from 1948): this contains records of births

of children with at least one parent normally resident in Scotland and deaths of Scottish residents on British-registered aircraft in any part of the world

- Service Records (from 1881): these include Army returns of births, deaths and marriages of Scottish residents at military service stations abroad, 1881–1959, and Service Department Registers, 1959 onwards, which record births, deaths and marriages of Scottish servicemen serving abroad and their families. There are also records of marriages performed by army chaplains abroad, from 1892 onwards, where one (or both parties) is Scottish and one (or both) parties is serving in the armed forces
- War Registers (1899 onwards): records of deaths of Scottish soldiers in the South African War (1899–1902), deaths of men, warrant officers, noncommissioned officers and petty officers serving in the army and the navy in the First World War (1914–18)
- Consular returns of births, deaths and marriages (1914 onwards): these are copies of registers of births, deaths and marriages of Scottish people held by British consuls abroad
- High Commissioners' returns of births and deaths (1964 onwards): these relate to births and deaths in Commonwealth countries of people who were Scottish by birth or descent. Limited records for some countries date back to earlier times, and some marriage returns are also available
- Register of births, deaths and marriages in foreign countries (1860–1965)

- Foreign marriages (1947 onwards): copies of some certificates of marriage of Scottish people who have married abroad according to the customs and laws of that country and without the presence of a British consular officer

Communications with New Register House by post should be made to the address on page 61. You may also make application by fax.

Ireland

Belfast

The central source for records of births, marriages and deaths in Northern Ireland is the General Register Office in Chichester Street, Belfast. Here are kept registers of births and deaths from 1 January 1864, and records of marriages from 1922. Records of non-Roman Catholic marriages from April 1845, and of all marriages from 1864 are held in the District Registrar's Offices.

The registers at the General Register Office are not open for public inspection, but the indexes may be searched for periods of six hours at a time, for a fee. Booking several months in advance is advised for this facility. You may carry out either a search over a five-year period or a general search, which is more expensive. For a fee, and provided that they are supplied with sufficient information to do so, staff at the General Register Office will carry out a search of the indexes for you for any particular event, searching over a period of five years, the year requested and two years either side. Apart from the general registers, the General Register Office also holds the following records of births, deaths and marriages:

- The Adopted Children Register: this contains records of all people adopted by court order in Northern Ireland from 1 January 1931
- The Marine Registers of births and deaths: these go back to 1922
- Consular returns of births and deaths: these are records of children born abroad to parents from Northern Ireland, and deaths abroad of people from Northern Ireland, registered by British consuls, from 1922
- Consular returns of marriages: records of people from Northern Ireland marrying abroad, registered by British consuls, from 1 January 1923
- Foreign Marriages: these records contain copies of certificates of marriages of people from Northern Ireland
- High Commissioner's returns of births, deaths and marriages: records of births, deaths and marriages registered by the British High Commissioner in Commonwealth countries
- Service Department Registers: these are records of births, deaths and marriages that were registered according to the Army Act of 1879 and date from 1 January 1927.

Enquiries to the Registrar General in Belfast may be made to the address on page 61.

Dublin
The General Register Office in Dublin holds records of all

births, marriages and deaths from 1864, and of non-Roman Catholic marriages since April 1845. Records held up until 1922 are for all of Ireland; thereafter they are for southern Ireland only, those for Northern Ireland being held in Belfast.

The address for the General Register Office in Dublin is on page 61.

The Census

The idea of a census, basically a head count of the population, goes back to ancient times. The New Testament tells us of Caesar Augustus ordering all men to return to their own towns to be taxed. Thus, we are told, Joseph had to take Mary to Bethlehem, and it was there that Jesus was born. This is the main purpose of censuses, which have been taken throughout the world in history—to compile information about the population, which government can use for administration and taxes.

The earliest example of such a record in England is the Domesday Book, which was compiled in 1086 under the authority of William the Conqueror. A regular count of the population did not, however, come into effect until 1801, largely because of public suspicion and opposition to such an idea. Since that year, a census has been taken every ten years in the United Kingdom, but the information that these records contain is not consistent, varying according to the wishes of the government in power at the particular time at which each census was taken. Moreover, no census was made in 1941, when the country was at war. Census records are subject to a law that prevents them from being accessible to public scrutiny for 100 years. The most recent census records that are available to the public, therefore, are those of 1891. The census for 1901 will be made public only after the year 2001.

It is generally accepted that the first census to be of any use to the family historian is that of 1841, although subsequent censuses are more informative.

The census for 1841 supplies the following information:

- The address of the household
- The names and surnames of each of the occupants of the house at that time
- The ages of each of the occupants; ages for children are precise, but for adults they are rounded to the nearest 5 years (thus 37 becomes 40, 54 becomes 50, etc)
- The occupations of the adults, within very broad definitions
- Place of birth; whether the person has been born within the county is indicated by yes or no. Births elsewhere are indicated by 'S' for Scotland, 'E' for England, 'I' for Ireland and 'F' for abroad, where relevant

The census of 1851 gives the following additional information:

- The relationship of each of the occupants of the house to the head of the household
- The exact ages of all occupants of the house
- Occupations of all adults
- The parish of birth of all occupants

- Marital status of all occupants, whether unmarried, married, widow or widower
- Whether born blind, deaf or dumb

The census of 1861 and subsequent censuses also contain information on the number of children in the household attending school, and the number of rooms in the house with more than one window.

Census Returns—England and Wales
The census returns for England and Wales, the Channel Islands and the Isle of Man are kept in the Public Records Office, Chancery Lane, London. If you acquire a reader's ticket, you can consult the microfilm copies. You may also apply to purchase a photocopy of the census entries that are of interest to you.

Census Returns—Scotland
The census returns for Scotland are available for consultation at New Register House in Edinburgh, and you may book to search the records there for a fee.

Census Returns—Ireland.
As a result of the damage caused by fire to the Four Courts in Dublin in 1922, very little remains of the census records until 1891. Census returns for 1901 and 1911 are, however, open to the public, and there are fragments of census returns from 1821–1851. The census returns may be consulted at the National Archives, Bishop Street, Dublin, or the Public Record Office of Northern Ireland, Balmoral Avenue, Belfast.

In order to be able to find your family in the census returns, you have to have a clear idea of at least the area in which they were likely to be living at the time. There will be information available in the form of leaflets or notices to help you to narrow your search down to the appropriate census enumeration district, but the more precise your knowledge is of the location of your family, the more likely you are to be able to find them in the records.

Census returns can help you to bridge the gap between the registers of births, marriages and deaths, and the parish records. For example, if you find out that John Green was 62 at the time of the census in 1851, you can then go on to search the parish registers around the time of his birth for an entry for his baptism. Remember, however, that if you are searching for such information about anyone who was an adult at the time of the 1841 census, you will have to search the parish records over a wider time scale, as the person's age in the census will only be accurate to the nearest five years.

Wills

If you are able to find copies of the wills of any of your ancestors, you might find that they make enlightening reading. You can glean all sorts of interesting information about your ancestors' circumstances from these documents. If a search through your family's mementoes does not reveal anything, there are various avenues that you can explore, although it is worth bearing in mind that until fairly recently will-making was very much the preserve of the well-off.

England and Wales

In England and Wales, the state was given the power of granting probate in 1858, and indexes of all wills since that period, compiled by the year and arranged alphabetically, can be consulted at the Principal Probate Registry, Somerset House, London. Indexes of letters of administration, where a person died intestate, are also included. You may consult the indexes free of charge, and you can pay to see copies of will documents. You may also, if you wish, purchase a photocopy of any will document that you want for your records.

The period before 1858 is more difficult as probate and administration was granted by ecclesiastical courts. In order to establish under which court's authority a particular will would come, it is necessary to establish whether or not the deceased was nonconformist, and where the deceased's property lay with regard to ecclesiastical boundaries. There are, however, books available that will guide you through the system (see the Useful Reading at the back of this book). Wills made under the jurisdiction of minor ecclesiastical courts are usually to be found in county record offices. Those made under the jurisdiction of the Prerogative Court of Canterbury, which covered counties in the south of England, can be found at the Public Record Office, Chancery Lane.

Wills and administrations made in Wales prior to 1858 are held in the National Library of Wales, Aberystwyth, Dyfed. You will need a reader's ticket to use the search rooms.

Scotland
If you wish to look up wills made in Scotland, start your search at the Scottish Record Office in Edinburgh. Many Scottish wills are kept there, and they will also be able to supply you with information on the holdings of wills elsewhere.

Northern Ireland
In Northern Ireland, indexes of wills are kept at the Public Record Office in Belfast, the address of which is given on page 61.

Republic of Ireland
In the Republic of Ireland, indexes of wills can be found

at the National Archives, Four Courts, Dublin, although Four Courts was severely damaged by fire in 1922, and many records were destroyed. Four Courts is not open to the public, but you may request, a day or two in advance, to inspect records from Four Courts at the National Archives reading room in Bishop Street.

Parish Records

Registers

For families belonging to the established church, the parish registers may prove an invaluable source for information pre–1837. Parish registers do not, as a rule, show dates of births and deaths, but instead they will show dates of baptisms and burials. Baptism dates will not necessarily be close to birth dates; some people were not christened until they were adults.

Before registration of births, marriages and deaths was enforced by the state, it was the local parishes who kept records of such events that occurred amongst their parishioners. In 1597 a rule was made that the entries of baptism, marriage and burial should be kept in a special register that should also contain any previous extant records going back to 1538, although some ministers thought that the new ruling extended back only as far as 1558, the year that Elizabeth Tudor came to the throne. Thus it is common to find that most surviving registers relate to years after 1558.

Until 1813 when the registers of the Church of England were standardized, parish records can be confusing. A little background knowledge is useful. England and Wales had around 11,000 parishes, differing quite considerably in extent, the largest of these being divided into chapelries, or chapels-at-ease. Many of these chapelries were given the right to hold their own baptism, marriage and burial services. Sometimes the chapelries kept their own records in a separate register and sometimes the information was recorded in the main parish register, often in a separate section. You will find it useful to consult *Guide to the Local Administrative Units of England* by F A Youngs.

The old custom of starting the official year on 25 March (Lady Day) rather than on 1 January can cause confusion. Dates relating to baptisms, marriages and burials that occurred between 1 January and 25 March, therefore, may require to have another year added to them. This method of dating records was changed on 1 January 1752, the year that Britain abandoned the Julian calendar in favour of the Gregorian calendar used by the rest of Europe.

In 1979 a ruling was made that all parishes should deposit their registers at the local record offices unless the relevant parish could prove that it could store and preserve the registers in good condition. Only a few parish records are now stored in parish churches, and even before the ruling of 1979 some parishes had voluntarily deposited their records in the local record offices because they either did not have the space or the facilities to store the registers themselves.

It is worth checking at the local reference library to see if the parish register that you are seeking is in print. Several parish registers were printed either privately or by a parish register society. Such societies can be up to a hundred years old, and some of them have several publications in print. If in fact the relevant parish register is not in print, you should visit the relevant record office where the registers are usually available for research on microfilm, as are the bishop's transcripts at the ancient diocesan offices (*see* page 44). The originals are not usually available because they are old and fragile and would deteriorate badly with a lot of handling.

Parish registers for Scotland are kept at New Register House. These registers are not complete, but for some parishes they date back as far as the late sixteenth century. Microfilm copies of parish registers are available for purchase. There is also a register of Neglected Entries, which lists births, deaths and marriages that were known to have taken place in Scotland between 1801 and 1854 but that were not recorded in the parish registers.

For Northern Ireland, consult the Public Record Office in Belfast. In Southern Ireland, the National Archives contain some Church of Ireland parish registers, although most of them are still in the possession of the local clergy. Some are also held by the Representative Church Body Library, Braemor Park, Dublin, and by the Public Records Office in Belfast. The National Archives in Dublin should be able to supply you with a list of all surviving parish registers, which amount to about one third of the parishes. A collection of Catholic records of baptisms, marriages and burials prior to 1880 can be consulted on microfilm in the National Library, Kildare Street, Dublin 2.

Some parish records and registers of nonconformists

for Wales can be consulted at the National Library of Wales, Aberystwyth, Dyfed, but a reader's ticket has to be applied for.

Before you embark upon a search of the parish registers, it is important to take account of the following:

- Parish Registers kept records of only those people who belonged to the established church
- In order to find your family in the parish registers, it is essential to know first of all which parish they lived in. If you cannot find records of your family in the parish to which you thought they belonged, it is worthwhile checking the records of surrounding parishes. Parish boundaries may have been changed through time
- Parish records were not always kept meticulously; there may well be inaccuracies and omissions. Omissions may not have been the fault of the priest of the parish; your ancestors may simply have failed to register

If you have had trouble locating records of some of your family members in the parish registers, it is worthwhile considering that the surname may have been spelt differently, or even that it was changed at some point in time. Check the records again, looking for similar-sounding names and seeing if they can be linked with your family through place of residence, named relatives, or family occupations. Complete name changes are harder to trace as there will be little evidence to prove family connections.

The form that recorded entries take varies considerably, and so, consequently, does the amount of information that you will be able to glean from them.

Finally, if you find your ancestors in the records of a parish some distance from where you live, you may then be led to visit the parish itself. Is the house in which your forebears lived still standing? Is there a family grave in the churchyard? Do you have any distant relatives still living in the locality? The parish records need not be the end of your search.

Tithe Records

These records can also be of use to the family historian. The church was entitled by law to one tenth of the produce of the land in its parish, and lists were kept of landowners and the amount for which they were liable. Consultation with the public record offices will generally reveal where to find records of tithe awards, or appointments.

Bishop's Transcripts

The 1597 ruling also decreed that in future a copy of baptisms, marriages and burials registered during the year should be sent to the local bishop. These are called Bishop's Transcripts, and they are available for research on microfilm at the archive offices of the ancient dioceses, e.g. York and Lincoln, which are different from the new dioceses created in the late nineteenth and twentieth centuries. This practice was kept up in England from the end of the sixteenth century until the late 1800s. These, when they are extant, are extremely useful as substitutes for the original where this has been lost or where it has been rendered illegible. Their accuracy, however, is not to be relied upon, depending as they did on the diligence and intelligence of the person transcribing the records; however, these documents can be helpful if they exist, in cases where parish records are missing.

Nonconformists

If your family did not belong to the established church, for example if they were Roman Catholic, Methodist, Quaker, Baptist or Jewish, you will need to take your search beyond the parish registers and look among registers of nonconformists. Some registers of nonconformists in England and Wales are kept at the Public Record office, some may be found in county record offices. Many Roman Catholic records have been lost or destroyed as a result of the secrecy under which the Catholics had to follow their religion in the sixteenth and seventeenth centuries. Consultation with the Catholic Record Society may help you in your search.

Records for the Quakers are quite comprehensive and indexes may be studied at the Society of Friends Library, Friends House, London.

Jewish records are kept, in general, in the care of the synagogues.

If you have no luck consulting records at the public or county record offices, you would be well advised to ask the relevant church authorities for advice.

It is sometimes the case that families belonging to nonconformist churches would have a child baptised twice, once within their own church and then again in the established church.

The International Genealogical Index

The International Genealogical Index, or IGI, is a computerized worldwide compilation of genealogical records made by the Church Jesus Christ of the Latter-Day Saints, or Mormons. They are interested in this kind of information because the Mormon Church's members have to trace their ancestors in order that they may be baptised by proxy but the International Genealogical Index is available to be consulted by anyone, whether or not he or she is a member of the Mormon Church. It is a tool of immense value to anybody interested in genealogical research. It is being added to all the time, but already has a vast amount of information on births and marriages available from countries all over the world. The library at Salt Lake City, in Utah in the United States, is the largest genealogical library in the world, but the church also has libraries in Britain, where you can look up the records or order records to be sent from Salt Lake City. They have huge collections of census returns, wills and other useful information.

The Index is available, free of charge or for a voluntary donation, in specially constructed buildings in various places throughout the country. Microfilm copies of the IGI are also available at some reference libraries and record offices, and the library catalogues of the Mormon's Family History Library are being made available on CD-ROM.

As with all research sources, however, there are some words of warning to be considered with reference to the IGI, For one thing, the index is far from being complete. This is partly because the sheer scale of the material is such that it is bound to take a long time to complete the consolidation of it. It is also partly because some Church of England clerics are unwilling to be involved in such a system because of their objections to people being baptised by proxy into the Mormon church when they had already been baptised by their parents into the Anglican faith. A point also worth remembering is that much of the material for the IGI has been collected by amateurs, who, although interested and enthusiastic, have no specialist training. All this does not detract, however, from the fact that the IGI can save you a lot of time that would be spent in consulting parish records directly.

Emigrants

Records of people leaving British shores for the colonies
are sketchy. Ships' passenger lists may be useful, although before the end of the nineteenth century they
were not kept on a regular basis. Passenger lists may be
found at the Public Record Office. If you believe that an
ancestor may have been transported as a criminal, it may
be worthwhile consulting the local history society in the
area from which your ancestors originated. They may
have records that could help you. Records in America of
immigrations after 1890 are quite good, but before that
time they are sparse. Information can be obtained from
the National Archives, Pennsylvania Avenue, Washington
DC. In Australia and New Zealand there are genealogical
societies that can be of help to you; some addresses for
these are given on page 62. Consular returns of births,
deaths and marriages abroad and High Commissioners'
returns of births, deaths and marriages for Commonwealth countries may also be of use to people researching their ancestors abroad. These records can help you to
establish the presence of your ancestors in the country
within a certain period of time. For example, if you find
an entry for the marriage of John Smith to Jane Brown in

India, entries in subsequent years for the births of their children, and then an entry for the death of John Smith in India some years later, you have some grounds for assuming that John Smith spent at least most of the intervening years in India.

Trades and Professions

If your ancestors belonged to certain trades or professions, you have a greater chance of finding information about them than if they were, for example, agricultural labourers. Census returns, particularly those of 1851 and after, tell you the occupation of adults in the family. If you found that they belonged to certain groups of professionals, you could take your research one step further. One of the easiest professions to trace is the clergy of the established church, those who had the task of keeping so many important records themselves. Many records of Church of England clergy can be found in county record offices, and there are also lists of clergy, such as the *Index Ecclesiasticum*, for the early nineteenth century, and *Crockford's Clerical Directory*, which dates from 1858. In Scotland, you may find it useful to look up *Fasti Ecclesiae Scoticanae*, or to consult the records of the Scottish Kirk Session, which are kept at New Register House. The clergy were generally a learned group of people, so it can also be worthwhile looking at the registers of universities.

Church leaders for other denominations or religions may be harder to trace, but it is worth inquiring from the relevant church authorities as to whether records are in existence that might be of use to you.

The medical profession is also easier to research than some. University registers can be useful, as can records of the Royal College of Physicians, or those of the Royal College of Surgeons.

Lawyers may also be traced through university registers, and those who rose to the higher echelons of the profession, such as barristers (advocates in Scotland) or judges, can generally be traced through court records.

Other records that may be helpful to you include trade and commercial directories, a collection of which may well be found in a reasonably large, well-equipped reference library. The drawback with these is that they are far from comprehensive since they have a tendency to concentrate on craftsmen, tradesmen and professional people in an area and ignore those who were unskilled workers, such as labourers or servants.

If any of your ancestors belonged to the services, there will almost certainly be a record of their existence somewhere, provided that it is not too far back in time. The sheer quantity of the records that are kept means that it is much easier to find your ancestors if they were officers. If your ancestor was in the army, the task of locating him will be greatly simplified if you know in which regiment he served. Regimental records of births, deaths and marriages are kept in the General Register Office at St Catherine's House. Most other Army records are kept in the Public Record Office, although some will be found in Army record offices. Officers can be found in the Army lists, which are kept in the Public Record Office at Kew, and which date back to the beginning of the nineteenth century. Following your ancestor's career can be made more interesting, if, having found out to which regiment he belonged, you can get a hold of a regimental history. Many such works have been written, and they can provide a valuable insight into Army life.

Lists of names of men liable for service, known as muster rolls or militia returns, were drawn up periodically from the sixteenth century to the nineteenth century. The muster rolls relating to Tudor and Stuart times are kept in the old Public Record Office at Chancery Lane in London with some being held in local record offices. A book that will prove useful if you wish to consult these is *Tudor and Stuart Muster Rolls: A Directory of Holdings in the British Isles* by Jeremy Gibson and Alan Dell. Another useful book is *Militia Lists and Musters 1757-1876: A Directory of Holdings in the British Isles* by Jeremy Gibson and Mervyn Medlycot.

Documentation for the Navy is every bit as plentiful as that for the Army. Records for the Admiralty are also kept in the Public Record Office, as are the records of the Royal Marines. With no regimental system to help you to narrow down your search, the quantity of these records can seem a little daunting, to say the least.

Before you embark on the task of finding ancestors who served in either the Army or the Navy, you would be well advised to read the guide to the Public Record Office, and also the publication by Cox and Padfield, *Tracing your Ancestors in the Public Record Office*, which should be available from bookshops of Her Majesty's Stationery Office (HMSO). There is also a printed list of

British National Archives that are held in the Public Record Office, which is published by HMSO.

At New Register House in Edinburgh, the following records are available that could be of use to those searching for ancestors in the Scottish military:

- Army returns for the period 1881–1959: births, deaths and marriages of Scottish people on military stations abroad
- War Registers, dating from 1899: deaths of Scottish soldiers in the South African War, 1899–1902; deaths of men and officers in the Army and Navy in the First World War (1914–18); deaths of Scottish armed forces' members in the Second World War (1939–45).

If your ancestor was killed in action, you may make enquiries to the Commonwealth War Graves Commission, who may be able to supply information as to where he was buried. The address for the Commonwealth War Graves Commission is given on page 61.

There are quite a few publications available on the subject of tracing ancestors in the Army or Navy, some of which are listed in the bibliography (*see* page 64).

It may be possible to find records of your ancestors for other professions as well. Many professions have associations or societies to which their practitioners belong, and some of these date back quite a long way in time. These associations may well hold some sort of historical records, as well as registers of members. Might your ancestor have served an apprenticeship? A central register of apprentices, dating back to the beginning of the eighteenth century, can be consulted at the Public Record Office.

Enquiries may lead you nowhere, but they are always worth making. The fuller the picture that you are able to build up of your ancestors, the more rewarding your task will prove to be.

Taking the Search Further

By the time you have mastered the art of searching through births, deaths and marriage registers, census returns, parish records, indexes of wills and the other records that have been mentioned already, you may feel that you have taken your work as far as you can. Should you wish, however, to continue your lines of research, there are many other avenues that you might like to explore, depending on the information you have accumulated so far about your family.

If you have been fortunate enough to be able to trace your family back as far as the sixteenth century, for example, there is a chance, albeit slim, that you may be able to find some manorial records still in existence that contain some mention of your family. If you make enquiries at the relevant county record office, they should be able to tell you whether such records have survived and, if so, where to find them. You will almost definitely need the assistance of someone with specialized knowledge; these records were written in Latin and are difficult to interpret.

Researching property deeds, dating back to the beginning of the eighteenth century in England, is another interesting but complicated way in which you can expand your knowledge. You can find out more about this by making enquiries at the Land Registry, Portugal Street, London.

Similar research in Scotland is slightly easier because of the existence of the Saisines Registers, which contain records of the transference of ownership of properties as far back as the sixteenth century in some cases. You will need expert help to find information in the Saisines Registers, which are kept at the Scottish Record Office—the old records were written by hand in Scots vernacular. Enquiries made to the Association of Genealogists (whose address is given on page 60) should lead you to someone who can assist.

Taxes, suffered by generation after generation, are well documented. Rates, income taxes, poll taxes, hearth tax, land tax, window tax—records for all these are in existence. Most are held in the Public Record Office, but some may be kept at local level. If you find your ancestors in tax returns, you can find out the address at which they lived, if you did not know before.

If any of your forebears did, or had done to them, something that could be deemed newsworthy, or if they plied a trade for which they might advertise in the paper, a large collection of English, Irish, Scottish and foreign newspapers, some of which date back to the early eighteenth century, is kept at the British Newspaper Library in London. Earlier newspapers, dating back to the beginning of the seventeenth century, are kept in the Burney Collection of newspapers in the British Library in London and in the Bodleian Library in Oxford.

Some local libraries will also hold copies of local newspapers dating back quite some way in time.

Your ancestors may have 'hit the headlines' for many reasons; one of those may have been that they committed some terrible crime. Court records can make interesting reading, and even if your ancestor was a petty offender, you may be able to locate his or her trial in court records in the public records office, either at local or central level. In England, the more serious offences were handled by the Assize courts, while the Quarter Sessions dealt with minor crimes. The records of the Assize courts can be found in the Public Records Office, while those of the Quarter Sessions should be available at county record offices.

Quarter Sessions records may also be of use to you if there were traders in your family; the Quarter Sessions dealt with shopkeepers' licences.

In the course of your search through your family's memorabilia, you may have been fortunate enough to find items such as school reports, books awarded as prizes for academic achievement, or school certificates; in this case, you will already have some knowledge about the education that some of your family received. But your information may contain gaps; for example, you may have found that your grandfather attended a certain school, but you still do not know whether his brothers and sisters went there as well.

If you wish to learn more about your ancestors' education and academic progress, you may find that the local school for the area in which they lived retains records of its former pupils going back to the founding of the establishment. If your family lived in a rural area it may be that the local school is no longer in existence, but it could be worthwhile checking in public records offices to see if the school registers have been retained.

The task that you have set yourself in finding out about the history of your family is certainly a complicated one, but, given time and patience, you should be rewarded with a fascinating stock of information about your predecessors. You can stop the search whenever you like, but no matter how far you take it, there will always be another piece of information somewhere, waiting to be unearthed. Good luck!

Useful Addresses

England

The Commonwealth War
  Graves Commission
2 Marlow Road
Maidenhead
Berks SL6 7DX
Telephone 01628 34221

Federation of Family History
  Societies
The Birmingham and Midland
  Institute
Margaret Street
Birmingham B3 3BS

Office of Population Censuses
  and Surveys
General Register Office
St Catherine's House
10 Kingsway
London WC2B 6JP

Postal Applications Section
Office of Population Censuses
  and Surveys
General Register Office
Smedley Hydro
Southport
Merseyside PR8 2HH

Principal Probate Registry
Somerset House
London

Keeper of the Public Records
Public Record Office
Chancery Lane
London WC2A 1LR
Telephone 0181 876 3444

The Public Record Office
Ruskin Avenue
Kew
Surrey TW9 4DU
Telephone 0181 876 3444

The Society of Genealogists
14 Charterhouse Buildings
Goswell Road
London EC1M 7BA
Telephone 0171 251 8799

The British Newspaper Library
Colindale Avenue
London NW9 5HE

The British Library
Great Russell Street
London WC1B 3DG
Telephone 0171 636 1544

Scotland

The Registrar General
New Register House
Edinburgh EH1 3YT
Telephone 0131 334 0380

The Scottish Record Office
HM General Register House
2 Princes Street
Edinburgh EH1 3YY
Telephone 0131 556 6585

The Scottish Genealogy Society
Victoria Street
Edinburgh EH1 2JL
Telephone 0131 220 3677

The Association of Scottish
 Genealogists and Record
 Agents
51/3 Mortonhall Road
Edinburgh EH9 2HN

The National Library of
 Scotland
George IV Bridge
Edinburgh EH1 1EW
Telephone 0131 226 4531

Northern Ireland

The Registrar General
Oxford House
49/55 Chichester Street
Belfast BT1 4HL
Telephone 0232 252000

Public Records Office (NI)
66 Balmoral Avenue
Belfast BT9 6NY
Telephone 01232 251318

The Irish Genealogical Project
2 Mellon Road
Omagh BT78 5QQ

The Irish Heritage Association
164 Kingsway
Dunmurry
Belfast BT17 2EJ

Republic of Ireland

The Registrar General
Joyce House
8/11 Lombard Street East
Dublin
Telephone 003531 671 1000

The National Archives
Bishop Street
Dublin 8
Ireland
Telephone 010 478 3711
(Most of the public records
for the Republic of Ireland
are now kept here. Records
that are still kept at Four
Courts can be consulted at
Bishop Street if notice is
given that you wish to use
them. Four Courts is not
open to the public.)

The Public Record Office of
  Ireland
Four Courts
Dublin 7

The Representative Church
  Body Library
Braemor Park
Dublin 14

The National Library of
  Ireland
Kildare Street
Dublin 2

Wales
The National Library of Wales
Aberystwyth
Dyfed SY23 3BU
Telephone 01970 623816

Australia
The Australian Institute of
  Genealogical Studies
P.O. Box 339
Blackburn
Melbourne
Victoria 3130

Genealogical Society of
  Victoria
Fifth Floor
252 Swanston Street
Melbourne
Victoria 3000

New Zealand
The New Zealand Society of
  Genealogists
P.O. Box 8795
Auckland 3

Useful Reading

General

First Steps in Family History by A. J. Camp—obtainable from the
  bookshop of the Society of Genealogists

Family History Beginner's Pack—obtainable from the bookshop
  of the Society of Genealogists

Beginning your Family History by G. Pelling

Everyone has Roots by A. J. Camp

The Family Tree Detective by C. D. Rodgers

Genealogy for Beginners by A. J. Willis and M. Tatchell

Tracing Your Ancestors in the Public Record Office by J. Cox
  and T. Padfield

The Oxford Guide to Family History by D. Hey

England

A comprehensive selection of publications relating to records
held at county or local level can be obtained from the
bookshop of the Society of Genealogists in London

English Genealogy by A. Wagner

English Ancestry by A. Wagner

Genealogical Sources in English Repositories by J. W. Moulton

*Church of England Ecclesiastical Courts: Their Officials and
  Their Records* by C. R. Chapman

Genealogical Research in England and Wales by F. Smith and
  D. E. Gardner

Guide to the Local Administrative Units of England by
  F. A. Youngs

Key to the Ancient Parish Registers of England and Wales by
  A. M. Burke
St Catherine's House Districts by R. Wiggins

Scotland

Guide to the Public Records of Scotland by M. Livingstone
Sources of Scottish Genealogy and Family History by D. J. Steel
Scottish Local History by David Moody
Surnames of Scotland by G. F. Black
Scottish Family History by M. Stuart

Ireland

The Ancestor Trail in Ireland by D. F. Begley
Handbook on Irish Genealogy by D. F. Begley
Tracing Your Irish Ancestors by J. Grenham

Wales

Welsh Family History: a Guide to Research by J. Rowlands

Overseas

The British Overseas by G. Yeo
*In Search of Your European Roots: a Complete Guide to Tracing
  Your Ancestors in Every Country in Europe* by A. Baxter

The Armed Services

Army Records for Family Historians by S. Fowler
*Militia Lists and Musters 1757–1876: A Directory of Holdings in
  the British Isles* by J. Gibson and M. Medlycot
Records of the Militia from 1757 by G. Thomas
Records of the Royal Air Force: How to Find The Few by E. Wilson
The Records of Naval Men by G. Fothergill
In Search of Army Ancestry by G. K. S. Hamilton-Edwards
*Tudor and Stuart Muster Rolls: A Directory of Holdings in the
  British Isles* by J. Gibson and A. Dell